A Teenager's Guide to

Living With An Alcoholic Parent

A Teenager's Guide to

Living
With An
Alcoholic
Parent

Edith Lynn Hornik-Beer

Hazelden

First published December, 1984.

Based on the book, You and Your Alcoholic Parent by Edith
Lynn Hornik
© 1974 by Association Press

ISBN: 0–89486–239–1

Printed in the United States of America.

Editor's Note:

Hazelden Educational Materials offers a variety of
information on chemical dependency and related areas. Our
publications do not necessarily represent Hazelden or its
programs, nor do they officially speak for any Twelve Step
organization.

About the book:
"Is Dad an alcoholic?" "Is it my fault Mom drinks?" "Why won't she just stop drinking?" "Where can I find someone to talk to?" "Where can we get help?" These are some of the questions teenagers have when living with alcoholic parents. This comprehensive guide answers questions for young people and discusses issues such as dating, school-work, expression of feelings, and responsibilities while coping with alcoholism at home.

About the author:
Edith Lynn Hornik-Beer is an independent writer who has written numerous books and articles for major periodicals and journals in the United States and Europe. For many years Ms. Beer wrote a weekly column for teenagers known as the *Young World.* Her writing is known for its extensive research combined with interviews with people reaching out for help. Ms. Beer specializes on issues such as teenagers, women, medicine, and health.

Preface

A Teenager's Guide to Living With an Alcoholic Parent is an abridged and updated version of the book, *You and Your Alcoholic Parent,* which was first published in 1974 by Association Press. The original book was written with the encouragement of Dr. Frank Seixas (at that time medical director of the National Council on Alcoholism) and Mrs. Judith Seixas, Yvelin Gardner, Dr. Mary Harper, Rita Rabinowitz, and Dr. Eva Rado. Others who helped me with the research and case histories were the late Dr. Ruth Fox, Barry Leach, the Reverend H. Gordon MacDonald, and Bernard Joseph. The real heart and soul of this book came from those Alateen groups who let me take part in their meetings and from those teenagers who confided their stories so that they may help other teenagers. Others who went out of their way to make this book possible were Alcoholics Anonymous, Al-Anon Family Group Headquarters, Westchester County Medical Society Library, and the National Council on Alcoholism library.

The updating and verification of the present book, *A Teenager's Guide to Living With an Alcoholic Parent,* was done with the help of Dr. Albert M. Browne-Mayers. My thanks go also to Alfred Taubman Medical Library, University of Michigan and Rutgers Center of Alcohol Studies Library.

Edith Lynn Hornik-Beer

Contents

Introduction

This is a book for those of you who are living with an alcoholic parent or parents.

You are well aware of the emotional impact alcoholism has on you and the perplexities, difficulties, and abuses you are faced with. You are probably seeking more information on how to manage your lives under such circumstances. You may wonder whom you can turn to and if they will understand the fear you live with at home. You worry whether your alcoholic parent will be abusive. Will he or she pass out? Will your mother forget to turn off the stove when alone in the house? Will you face another lonely evening because your father sits in glum silence with his liquor bottle as his sole companion?

In writing this book it has been my object to define in realistic, concrete, and nontechnical language the essential facts of alcoholism and what you, as a young person, experience under such circumstances.

For many years I have had the opportunity to teach creative writing and to write for teenagers. My writing led me to wherever young people might be: the Youth Consultation Services, teenage walk-in centers, Family Service, hospitals, Alateen, police headquarters, courts, and all kinds of schools—private, parochial, and public.

Whenever a real problem came up, such as a teenager

dropping out of school in despair or turning to hard drugs in anger and pain, too many of the cases could be reliably traced to alcoholism. Those who came from alcoholic homes showed signs of having been abused, mistreated, and often neglected. They were subject to mental depression and had feelings of guilt and inferiority. All too many had not been helped to recognize that their immediate personal difficulties related to the parental alcoholism at home. These youngsters knew only that they had lost confidence in themselves, in the community, and in their parents. But once the source of the problem was discovered, these young people wanted more and more answers to their questions about alcoholism; and with the answers came a certain amount of relief from the disruption in their lives.

This book is a composite record of all those questions young people have asked in my presence and is based largely on their experiences with parental alcoholism.

My aim in this book is to talk about how alcoholism affects young people who have to live with it. I have attempted, with a question and answer format, to get down to such practical problems as: How can I change the situation, or how can I get help? How can the family get help? How do I bring a friend home when my parent is drunk? What do I do if my alcoholic parent hits me or insults me unfairly?

No matter how upsetting these problems are to you personally, they all tie in with the fact that alcoholism is a disease; the alcoholic is a sick person, and you are affected by his or her illness.

It's important to know that you are not alone. The United States Public Health Service ranks alcoholism—along with heart disease, cancer, and mental illness—as one of the four greatest public health problems in the country. It is estimated that there are over ten million alcoholics in the United States. That is more than the total population of many nations. For example, Switzerland has a population of six million and Norway has less than four million. There are enough alcoholics in the United States to form a small nation.

If you count the sons, daughters, husbands, and wives affected by living with the ten million alcoholics, the number of those hurt by alcohol multiplies to about forty million. Alcoholic parents, once they are recovering, regain their original intelligence, sensitivity, and pleasantness. You may be too young to know what your alcoholic parent was like before he or she became ill.

The answer to living with alcoholism, as it is to any other disease, is knowledge. Learning about alcoholism will help those of you living with an alcoholic parent. This knowledge may bring you new hope, courage, and peacefulness.

Editor's Note:
The pronouns have been alternated throughout the text in order to avoid the cumbersome use of he/she. This should in no way imply stereotyping of any behaviors to either sex.

1

Alcoholism

What is alcoholism?
Alcoholism is an illness. Alcoholics are as sick as people who have tuberculosis or diabetes. People who are alcoholics are excessive drinkers. They cannot always stop at one or two drinks. Most alcoholics start out with the same intentions as the nonalcoholic: to have no more than one or two drinks. The nonalcoholics, or so-called social drinkers, can stop when they choose. Alcoholics cannot stop. For alcoholics, drinking becomes a compulsion. They are victims of their own compulsion.

How does alcoholism start?
Doctors just don't know why people become alcoholics. Some start out as social drinkers, and then become, for some reason that physicians have not yet been able to define, physically dependent on alcohol. A person may become an alcoholic if she drinks regularly to forget a problem, to quiet unpleasant, nagging feelings, or to calm nerves. As with alcoholics who drink to stifle their unhappy feelings, persons physically dependent on alcohol become nervous and unhappy and lose control over their lives and actions. Whatever the reason, once alcoholics start to drink they are unable to stop at will.

Is it the number of times a person drinks each week or the quantity of alcohol consumed that describes an alcoholic?

Neither, there may be periods—of weeks or months—when an alcoholic does not drink. The important point is that *when* alcoholics drink they lose control of their actions. The drinking may eventually damage them physically and mentally. It can keep them from performing their job and from getting along with family and with the neighbors.

If alcoholics know they can't drink, why don't they just get hold of themselves and stop drinking?

Giving up alcohol is very hard for alcoholics, and it does not happen overnight. The desire to drink is strong and they cannot control it. Most alcoholics cannot give up drinking on their own; they need help, as any other sick person needs help.

I feel if I could just keep my parent from seeing alcohol he would give it up. Should I throw out all the bottles in the house?

Many teenagers have wanted to throw out the liquor in the house or ask friends not to drink in the alcoholic's presence. This will not solve the problem. You cannot prevent the alcoholic from coming close to alcohol any more than you can prevent a diabetic from seeing sweets. The problem is within the person and not in that bottle of alcohol.

If the alcoholic needs help, why doesn't she go to a doctor?

In the early stages of alcoholism, alcoholics are usually not aware they are ill. Alcoholism is a progressive illness. Even when the alcoholic becomes aware that all is not well, she may still be the last one to connect the illness with drinking.

Why do some people vomit when they drink alcohol?
Alcohol irritates the lining of the stomach. It is this
irritation which causes the gagging, nausea, and vomiting.
There also can be an effect on the vomiting center in the
brain.

What is meant by "passing out"?
Passing out is a loss of consciousness.

What causes this loss of consciousness?
Alcohol decreases the function of the brain and can
cause a loss of consciousness. Too much alcohol can paralyze
the respiratory center of the brain and cause not only unconsciousness but death. However, when a person drinks often
enough, and in large enough quantities, the brain becomes
"used to," or adapted to, alcohol so that large amounts
may be taken without causing unconsciousness or death.
The family of the alcoholic should be aware that using
alcohol with other drugs can cause a person to pass out,
or, in some cases, death may result. Sleeping pills or tranquilizers, since their effect lasts longer when mixed with
alcohol, can cause the alcoholic to pass out. Such a situation
might be very serious even if he is used to alcohol.
Furthermore certain metabolic conditions such as diabetes or cirrhosis of the liver can cause unconsciousness even
without alcohol. And the problem can be greatly aggravated
by the use of large amounts of alcohol. It is good for everyone in the family to know if the alcoholic has such a sickness
so that if he were found unconscious, the family would
be able to inform the attending doctor.

What is a blackout?
When a person drinks heavily and steadily and the brain
becomes adapted to alcohol, she does not become unconscious as quickly as you or I would. In fact, she may act
in a perfectly sober manner, but will have periods of time

7

during which she has a loss of memory. *Blackout* is the term used to describe this temporary loss of memory due to drinking.

Unless you have reason to ask the alcoholic if she remembers, you have no way of knowing whether she had a blackout. Sometimes the alcoholic will attempt to cover up for this memory loss because it is embarrassing. Usually the loss of memory is total and she will completely deny the events that took place while the blackout was occurring.

While driving a car, the alcoholic may have hit another car and not remember the accident. If you know about blackouts, you will understand that this person is probably being as honest as she can when saying, "I don't remember." You will just have to accept this answer as the truth.

Do certain types of families tend toward alcoholism?

According to the National Council on Alcoholism, various studies have shown that, among others, the following factors may place a family or family member in a high-risk category:

—a history of alcoholism;
—a history of teetotalism (no drinking of alcoholic beverages);
—alcoholism or teetotalism in the family of one of the parents;
—the experience of a broken home;
—parental discord, or a parent who was nonpunitive, absent, or rejecting;
—being the last child in a large family;
—family members with a high incidence of recurrent depression for more than one generation.

Can a teenager be an alcoholic?

Some teenagers are already alcoholics, and those teenagers who are drinking heavily are at a greater risk for alcoholism later on. It is known that heavy drinkers and problem drinkers tend to start drinking in their teens.

Are teenagers today starting to drink at a younger age?

When compared to thirty years ago, more young people are drinking at an earlier age and are prone to developing excessive and acute alcohol use.

What is excessive and acute alcohol use?

There are different drinking habits among teenagers. Some teenagers drink regularly. Other teenagers and youths may drink less regularly, but when they drink, they tend to consume larger amounts. These large amounts (or excessive and acute alcohol use) cause acute problems ranging from traffic fatalities to other alcohol-related injuries. Furthermore, both the teenagers who drink regularly and those who drink occasionally but excessively, make themselves sick and are often impaired and unable to concentrate. Their drinking habits may keep them from completing their education and reaching the goals they desire.

Do all drinking teenagers become alcoholics?

Some "mature out" and do not become problem drinkers. A recent study has shown that adolescents with "problem behavior" have a higher risk of becoming problem drinkers as adults.

What is "problem behavior"?

Problem behavior may include alienation from school, teachers, religion, or positive moral beliefs. Other problems include use of alcohol and other drugs and inappropriate sexual behavior. Teenagers who seek help from counselors or religious groups, in order to deal with their problems and set goals, may change their whole life in a positive way.

Is using alcohol with marijuana dangerous?

Using alcohol and marijuana together is twice as dangerous as only drinking. Tests have shown that abilities and health were more impaired with alcohol and marijuana combined than with either drug alone.

Is it less dangerous to take tranquilizers than to drink?

All drugs can be dangerous and addictive unless carefully prescribed by a physician. One physician in the field of alcoholism has called careless pill taking "eating your alcohol."

2

Are you sure you have an alcoholic in your family?

Is all drinking bad?
Not all drinking is bad, nor does all drinking lead to alcoholism.

Many people drink to be sociable. They may have one or two cocktails before dinner. Or they may have a few drinks at a party to relax. But they know when to stop, and they have no trouble stopping. They may occasionally have one too many, but their drinking is not continual or habitually excessive.

Others drink to enhance their eating experience. Many a gourmet would not touch a roast beef without the proper accompanying glass of red wine, nor would she consider a good fish dinner complete without the correct white wine.

Some nations take pride in their national drink. Germany is associated with beer, France with wines and champagnes, and Russia with vodka. When traveling, many tourists enjoy each country's drink without any harm to themselves.

Some of us are accustomed to seeing alcohol used in religious rituals. It's interesting to note that alcohol was one of the earliest forms of medicine.

How can I tell if my parents are really alcoholics or if I am only imagining they are drinking too much?

If you wonder whether you have an alcoholic at home, react to these statements. Check the proper response to each.

	YES	NO
1. One or both of my parents have alcohol on their breath before 10 A.M.	___	___
2. One or both of my parents do not bother to eat regular meals and drink instead.	___	___
3. One or both of my parents do not remember what they said or did or what happened to them after they slept off the effects of their drinking.	___	___
4. One or both of my parents do not spend time mixing cocktails or comment on how the drinks taste but gulp down many drinks straight.	___	___
5. One or both of my parents have to take a drink when asked to make a decision.	___	___
6. One or both of my parents, on occasion, stay intoxicated for several days.	___	___
7. One or both of my parents get intoxicated on working days.	___	___
8. I discover hidden bottles of alcohol in the most unlikely places in our home such as under a pillow, behind the couch, or in the bathroom.	___	___

If you reacted with a yes to one or more statements, you may have someone in your home with the symptoms of alcoholism.

Is there a particularly good time to discuss the problem of alcoholism with a drinking parent?

It is difficult to tell a person he is an alcoholic if he has not yet realized he drinks excessively. It is especially difficult for a son or daughter to tell a parent that he is an alcoholic. If you start to diagnose your parent's illness, he might feel you are acting out of place. Thus, without meaning to, you might hurt his feelings and affect your future relationship.

When a parent drinks, try not to get into a conversation. Anyone who is under the influence of alcohol won't know what he is saying or doing. Stay out of the way. This is not the moment to tell him he's an alcoholic. He simply cannot understand.

When your parent is in the process of sobering up, he will feel ill. This is the moment to talk to him if you can find it within your heart to show sympathy. You might tell him how worried, concerned, frightened, and helpless you felt while he was drinking. You might also ask if he would like to talk to a doctor, to a clergyperson, or someone from Alcoholics Anonymous.

Such comments from you will help your parent realize that you are treating the drinking not as a disgrace but as an illness. Because they feel so ill, many alcoholics have at such moments been willing to see a doctor, or a fellow alcoholic who has succeeded in arresting his drinking and knows how miserable the alcoholic feels.

Alcoholics are extremely sensitive people, and if you preach to them or make them feel guilty about their illness, they will not listen to you. An alcoholic needs love and approval.

If you have a mother or father who refuses to give up drinking, and refuses to recognize that he or she is ill, try to divorce yourself emotionally from the drinking. You can still have respect for your parent when he or she is sober, but keep telling yourself that the problems drinking causes are basically theirs. No one can *make* a parent give up drinking. A person has to want to give up drinking. You can hope that your parent will slowly come to see the situation as it really is.

My parents are divorced. My mother works in a department store. Almost every night she comes home smelling of alcohol and continues to drink all evening. When I mention the alcohol to her, she pretends she doesn't drink at home and says she only had one drink at work because she had to entertain an important customer. If I tell her I don't believe her, she tells me I am fresh. Is my mother an alcoholic?

Yes. Your mother's excuses as to "why I *had* to drink" are typical symptoms of alcoholism. Alcoholics are so frightened about their drinking, what their drinking is doing to them, and their lack of control once they do drink that they minimize the amount of alcohol they take and put the emphasis on *why* they had to drink. In a sense they are saying, "It is not my fault—politeness forced me to drink." So, you see, this is your mother's way of rationalizing her drinking to you and even more to herself. Your mother's need to be respected by you causes her to tell you that drinking is an important asset on her job. She is embarrassed that you know she is drinking.

I brought home a friend from school. My mother offered to make us a peanut butter sandwich. She was so intoxicated that she spread the peanut butter on the table instead of on the bread. I was so embarrassed that when my friend left I screamed at my mother, asking her why she had to drink. My mother said she drinks because she needs a pick-me-up, feels depressed, and has many troubles and worries. I can't see what her worries are. My father supports us and is good to us. Are her feelings part of alcoholism?

14

Alcohol causes anxiety and depression. Many of your mother's emotional ups and downs would not be so great if she were able to give up alcohol. She uses her emotions as a reason for drinking. It is the drinking that is causing her extreme behavior. Once your mother realizes she is using alcohol as a crutch for her intense emotions, and is able to examine these emotions, she may be able to accept alcoholism as an illness.

My father often gets intoxicated. Each time he gets drunk, he promises not to drink again. My father says any man who promises not to drink can stop drinking. Why hasn't he stopped drinking?

Your father's promises to stop drinking are one of the symptoms of alcoholism. When your father promises not to drink again, he honestly feels he can keep that promise. When your father takes that first drink, he feels that with a little discipline he can control his drinking. Deep down he is frightened that he cannot. He is most likely wondering what has happened to him. He keeps asking himself if he could be losing his mind. Until your father understands that alcoholism is an illness, he will feel bewildered and upset that he cannot control his drinking.

My father only drinks when something goes wrong at the office. Is that alcoholism too?

Anyone who drinks to solve a problem or because his day did not go right may become an alcoholic. However, it depends on how your father drinks. Does his drinking get out of control, or does he have only one or two drinks? Does he always drink when something goes wrong in his life or only after a hard day's work? Review the eight statements listed earlier in this chapter to make sure you are not jumping to conclusions.

15

3

Blackouts, unkept promises, unfair criticism, and family arguments

Why do some alcoholics make unrealistic promises when they drink?

An alcoholic, when drinking, is apt to make all kinds of promises to the family. The alcoholic parent may promise a new car, a much-wanted trip, a phone of your own in your room. An alcoholic makes such promises under the influence of alcohol in the hope of gaining the family's love and respect her deflated ego desperately craves. The alcohol helps the parent feed the fantasy of what he or she would like to be able to do for the family and the kind of person she would like to be.

Why do some alcoholics, when drinking, criticize their children unfairly?

When an alcoholic criticizes or even insults the children unfairly, it is because that parent wants to be looked upon as a big, powerful, wonderful person and a successful parent.

Deep down, the alcoholic hates himself and is suffering from this self-hate and guilt. To get relief the alcoholic projects these self-critical feelings (such as "I am no good," . . . "I am weak, a sissy") onto the nearest person. Remember, it may be feelings like these that trigger him to drink.

My mother is an alcoholic who never stops hurting our feelings. Is she aware she is insulting or making unrealistic promises to her family while under the influence of alcohol?

Most likely your parent, once she is sober, will not remember what she said or did. Alcohol is an anesthetic. When used over a long period of time, it can cause lapses of memory, known as blackouts.

Can an alcoholic parent's unfair criticism affect me?

If you have been subject to unfair criticism from birth it can discourage you from using your talents to the fullest, from completing chores and school work. As an adult, it can even discourage you from going into a profession.

Give an example of a teenager who became discouraged by unfair criticism from his alcoholic parent.

Stuart is a typical sixteen-year-old boy who experienced and suffered from the criticism of an alcoholic parent. It seemed to Stuart the only thing his father ever had to say to him was, "You haven't got a brain in your head." Stuart was a sophomore in high school. It was true he was a poor student, or what his dean called an "underachiever." Even though Stuart knew he was an underachiever, he would have liked to hear his father say, just once, something else when he brought home his report card other than his usual, "You haven't got a brain in your head."

Stuart was determined to prove to his father he did have a brain in his head. Stuart studied very hard. Some nights it was difficult for him to concentrate on his homework because he could hear his parents bickering in the next room.

"You forgot to pay the mortgage again. The bank is fed up."

"How many times can a person smash up a car? I'm surprised they haven't taken your license away!"

"If you wouldn't drink so much. . ."

Stuart didn't like the bickering, and wondered if his parents might separate. He wondered, too, because his father was so forgetful about paying the bills, if they might lose their home.

He kept telling himself that if he studied hard, maybe, by some miracle, things would get better at home.

Stuart's determination to concentrate on his school work, in spite of the bickering and worries at home, paid off. His next report card showed a marked improvement. There was even a personal note of praise from his dean written on the report card.

Proudly Stuart put the report card on his father's desk. Stuart felt happier than he had felt in a long time. He knew that his father could only be pleased with such a report, but more important, maybe now his father would realize that he was intelligent and would start paying some attention to him. Stuart could remember when his father used to go to ballgames and movies with him. Who knew? Maybe things would go back to the way they used to be. Stuart would offer to get a part-time job to help pay off some of the bills. He thought that might lessen some of the arguing at home and keep the family from breaking up. He would let his father know that he was old enough to understand things weren't always easy at the office.

When Stuart's father came home and saw the report, he said without any hesitation, "Well, well, who did the work for you? I know you don't have the brains to do it!"

Stuart was stunned. All that work for nothing! He wouldn't be surprised if his father not only thought he was stupid but hated him, too.

Stuart would not have been as hurt if he had only known his father was tied up in his own miserable feelings. This kept him from recognizing what Stuart had accomplished in school.

Do these alcoholic parents understand how they hurt their children?

Sometimes the parents do understand but do not know how to help themselves. Alcoholic parents are what they are because of their personality makeup and not because they want to hurt their children or be purposely unpleasant.

Where can one go when a parent drinks?

Go for a walk. Do your homework in the library. Visit a good friend, go to Alateen, a teenage walk-in center, community center, or get involved in after-school activities.

My father is an alcoholic. He usually drinks several days in a row. Should I stay away during these days?

If you can, yes. Stay with a favorite aunt, cousin, or grandmother. Be sure that your mother knows where you are at all times. Your nondrinking parent, or the adult in charge of the alcoholic, has enough problems without having to worry about where you might be.

What can a teenager do if the alcoholic parent becomes nasty and insulting?

The problem of living with an alcoholic parent will become simplified if you can avoid a confrontation while your parent is drinking. Just keep telling yourself that your parent is ill and that her true self is not speaking to you. Not fighting back will conserve your strength for better things. If you must answer back, give an answer like, "I am your daughter (or son) and I love you." It may shock your parent into a moment of silence.

Of course, if you are insulted, once in a while you are going to show your irritation. Don't worry about it. Once in a while that won't be harmful for you or your parent. Just keep trying to detach yourself emotionally from what a drinking parent may unknowingly say. Remember, your alcoholic parent will not recall what was said once she recuperates. In most cases it is desirable to avoid seeing a parent in an alcoholic state. It will be easier for you to accept that parent when she is sober. The best thing to do when a parent is drinking excessively is to get out of the house.

How can we avoid repeating our families' mistakes?

Problems are a part of everyone's life, and the clue to coping with them is to understand ourselves and our environment. This means taking a close look at ourselves, but it's worth it. Only if we know why we act and feel the way we do will we be freed from repeating our families' mistakes.

Is it true that some alcoholics are very quiet while actively drinking, and it is their children who start to fight with the alcoholic?

Sometimes youngsters are so angry at their parent's drinking that they pick a fight to "get back at him." It makes these youngsters angry that their parent cannot be responsive when they need him to give the parental attention they want and deserve.

Should one stay away from every discussion with the alcoholic parent—even when she is not drinking?

When your parent is not drinking, listen to her. You may find that she has some good things to say. Children who have an alcoholic in their midst have to learn to tell the difference between sober discussions, thoughtful adult criticism, and those arguments caused by the drinking.

What are sober arguments, sober criticism, and sober discussion?

Sober arguments, as referred to in this book, are those discussions in a family that are caused not by alcoholism but by normal day-to-day life. For instance, if the alcoholic parent complains that his son or daughter stays out too late at night, he may have a valid concern which has nothing to do with his drinking.

In some families the children are so used to ignoring the alcoholic parent that they might be tempted to dismiss the alcoholic's concern with a "but you drink" retort. It is unfair to the alcoholic and a good way to avoid an important but inconvenient subject.

Don't forget that alcoholics drink to escape unpleasant feelings about themselves. If you can, when the alcoholic is sober, make him feel an important part of the family. This may motivate him to learn about the illness.

My mother loses her temper when my father drinks. I don't blame my mother, and I take her side. My father gets furious with me for what he calls interfering. Wouldn't you think, as a daughter, I have the right to interfere?

We are often tempted to take sides when parents argue. Parents argue because they have reached the limit of their patience. When you take sides, it gives them more reasons to argue, and one parent may feel that you are teaming up against him or her. Teenagers usually take the side of the parent who they feel protects them and who they feel may be threatened. Before getting involved in your parents' argument, decide what can be accomplished by interfering. Too often, such interference may lead to further isolation from one parent.

Both my parents are alcoholics. When they argue, they ask me for my opinion. Consequently, without wanting to, I get involved in their arguments. How can I get them to leave me alone?

Answer them honestly. "I would like to help you, but I don't know how." If that does not work, go for a walk.

4

Your alcoholic parent's job

I am afraid my father will lose his job because he drinks. How can we help him hide his drinking in the hope that his company won't notice it?
Very often, out of fear that the alcoholic may lose his job, the alcoholic's family will help him hide his drinking from the world. If he has a hangover, the family may think they are helping him out by calling his company and telling them he won't be in because he has a "cold" or a "virus." An employer soon sees through such excuses.

When a family makes excuses for the alcoholic, they are in a sense allowing the illness to progress. Deep down, the alcoholic feels he can drink because the family will help by covering up for him. The alcoholic will not recognize drinking as an illness because the family is hiding it as a disgrace instead of openly declaring it as a problem that can be treated.

When a company recognizes it has an alcoholic employee, is it likely that the alcoholic will eventually lose the job?
Not necessarily. Some companies have excellent programs to help the alcoholic. Rather than fire the alcoholic because the drinking keeps her from working at full capacity, the medical department, the personnel department, or the boss will inform the alcoholic that a deterioration in

her work has been noticed. A medical checkup or professional counseling may be suggested. The doctor will question the parent about her drinking habits and inform her about alcoholism. The doctor or counselor may suggest steps for the alcoholic to take to help and explain what resources the company or the community offers.

Very often a boss can get the alcoholic to accept the problem more readily than the family can. Deep down, she is afraid of losing a job. When a boss speaks to the alcoholic, she can no longer fool herself, and this may motivate her to seek professional help.

In that case, isn't it fair to tell my father's company that he drinks?

Definitely not. Your father's drinking is an illness, and he has to take the steps to help himself. Your best course of action is not to interfere.

My father is an alcoholic. What will happen to our family if he should lose his job?

Financial problems can become serious for the family. It may be necessary to seek outside help. While this is not pleasant to think about, it is also true that such a situation may shock the alcoholic into realizing that he is ill and must have help to deal with his illness.

My father is an alcoholic who lost his job due to his drinking. My mother has taken a job. My father has still not given up drinking or sought help. What can we do?

Your family can do a lot to help your father. Your father is, most likely, unhappy that he has lost his job. He may rationalize that it wasn't the drinking that cost him his job, but something else, such as a lack of ability. He can use such illusions as an excuse to drink. The family should try to bolster your father's ego and make him realize that it was not his lack of capabilities as a breadwinner that made him lose his job; it was his illness. He should be made to feel that he is a worthwhile, talented man who is capable of gaining his health back. Once your father sees his situation in the proper light, he will hopefully seek out A.A., a clinic, a hospital, or other facilities which offer help and hope for recovery.

My mother is an illustrator of children's books. After she finishes a project she always drinks too much. Why is that?

The alcoholic drinks to suppress emotional discomfort. Your mother may be a perfectionist who feels inadequate about even her best work as an artist. Some alcoholics rationalize that their finished piece of work deserves a celebration and reward themselves by going on a drinking binge. Or, it is possible that your mother feels insufficient as a human being and that these feelings were temporarily repressed during the period of artistic creativity.

Many successful people have become alcoholics for similar reasons. Did you know, for example, that such famous writers as O. Henry, Stephen Crane, Sinclair Lewis, F. Scott Fitzgerald, Eugene O'Neill, and Edna St. Vincent Millay were all alcoholics?

5

Problems faced by your nonalcoholic parent

Does every parent who lives with an alcoholic spouse suffer from strain and tension?

Yes. Any parent who lives with an alcoholic spouse has many emotional burdens and much pressure to bear.

What are some of these pressures and emotional burdens?

The parent who lives with the alcoholic is continually nagged by worry. How can he protect the children from the drinking parent? The sober parent has to make decisions alone regarding their children and wonders what alcoholism will do to the family's economic status. He may wonder if the children will be able to finish school or if the family will have to move.

The nonalcoholic parent has to face the loss of friends who do not want to deal with the ups and downs of an alcoholic. The nonalcoholic parent has to try to explain to relatives, who know nothing about alcoholism, what has happened in their home. The nonalcoholic parent lacks companionship in the evening and has to take over the chores which the alcoholic parent would normally undertake. The parent living with an alcoholic spouse can never plan anything confidently.

My father is an alcoholic. My mother seems perfectly relaxed to me.

Your nonalcoholic mother may act with sureness and capability, on the surface, as an attempt to protect you and to keep your home together. But, deep down, she is anxious about all she has to take care of.

Can all these emotions complicate the relationship between the nondrinking parent and the children?

Yes. In many cases, parents who live with the extreme anxiety caused by alcoholism cannot express their true thoughts. In some instances yelling at the nearest member of the family becomes an outlet for pent-up feelings. Deep down they are ashamed of themselves for yelling and are wondering what is happening to them. There are times when the nonalcoholic parent worries if she, too, is becoming ill.

My mother, who is an alcoholic, will put up with anything we want. My father who is not an alcoholic is always in a bad mood. He says my mother spoils us. Why can't my father be a better sport?

What your father is trying to tell you is that, while your mother permits you to do anything to gain her love, he is left with the unpleasant task of saying no when the need arises. This does not always endear him to you. When your father does not get the cooperation and the understanding he deserves for his decisions and actions, he may become ill-tempered.

Remember, too, that your father may be extra tense if he has to go to work and leave the house in the charge of your alcoholic mother. He knows that his children may come home from school to a locked door and that your alcoholic mother may be lying unconscious within the house. He knows that you may be ashamed to bring home friends because of your mother's behavior. He worries whether the refrigerator will be empty at dinner time because the household money was spent on liquor. You can ease the tension at home by trying to understand your father's position and offering to cooperate with him in every way possible.

My father is an alcoholic who lost his job. My mother is now supporting us. We thought, once Mom had a steady job, our lives would be easier. Why have our lives become more complicated instead, and why do we argue more than ever before?

In any home, any illness, not just alcoholism, can upset interfamily relationships because the roles get shifted around. The older son may, for instance, have to give up a club meeting or a ball game to take care of the younger children. Your mother can't drive you to the pool or to a friend's house because she has to go to work. Conversely, if a mother is the alcoholic, a father can't relax on the weekends with his children because he has extra responsibilities.

The family has to recognize that money for a second family car, a vacation, or an evening out may be spent on medical care.

Unless the family understands the situation, the pressure can cause almost unbearable emotional chaos.

Your best course of action is to sit down as a family and make a schedule of your chores, allowing leisure time for each member of the family, including your parent who works.

My mother has left my father, who is an alcoholic. She works and I try to help her. But she is unreasonable. If I am out playing baseball with the guys, she'll call me off a base just to put the laundry in the drier. Is this type of behavior fair?

No, it is not fair. Your mother acts this way because she is so tired that it's hard for her to get up from her chair to put the laundry in the drier. A contributing factor to your mother's tiredness is the fact that she suppressed her problems while on the job all day. She cannot discuss with everyone her many worries and her loneliness. A simple, straightforward reply to your mother's unexpected requests may avert an argument. Try saying, "May I do it as soon as I come in? I joined this game before I knew you had a chore for me." You'll discover if you really do the chore later, your mother will be more likely to trust you to schedule your own work.

I understand that my mother has to work and may be tired. Sometimes when I stay around the house to help, she will explode and shout, "Get out of the house, go visit your friends!" How am I to know what to do?

Teenagers who live in a home where there is alcoholism complain frequently about one of the parents exploding for no reason in particular. When we live with tension, we become explosive. Since most of us would be embarrassed to burst out in public, we let it out mostly on those we love.

While your mother does sound harsh, all she is saying is, "I had a hard day in the office. Conferences, dictation, constant chatter. I can't take any more, not even affection." This does not mean that you should really get out of the house as your mother requested. If you stay, you may find that what your mother really wants is someone to talk to.

My mother is an alcoholic. I am a sixteen-year-old girl, and my father worries about me unduly. If I go to a girlfriend's house, he worries if I will be safe, if it is safe for me to walk home alone, and if I will have a drink while I am out. Why does my father worry more than other fathers?

A parent who lives with an alcoholic spouse has so many real fears that worrying becomes a habit in his daily life. It can cause negative thinking and result in parents worrying too much about their children. In your case, where your mother is the alcoholic, it is not unusual for a father to worry that his daughter will take after her mother and drink, too. There have been many cases in which a child was the "spitting image" of his alcoholic parent, and the nondrinking parent assumed that this child would take after the alcoholic parent.

Of course such an assumption on the part of a parent would be unfair. As a parent in this position learns more about alcoholism, and, hopefully, goes to Al-Anon or counseling, such fears should ease.

In the meantime, you can reassure your father by being supportive. Let your father know where you are going, what you are doing. Phone him if you are going to be late. If he expresses a fear, talk it over with him even if it is a far-fetched fear.

31

6

Let's take a good look at ourselves

My mother is an alcoholic. I am so frightened when she drinks that there are times when I can't sleep, and I can't concentrate in school. What can I do to calm myself?

The constant fear that comes from living with an alcoholic parent can exhaust and wear all family members down. This is why alcoholism is called the "family disease."

You will find your difficulties less scary if you have an objective person to talk to. All members of a family who have an alcoholic in their midst should never hesitate to talk to their clergyperson, an Alcoholics Anonymous member, to someone from Al-Anon or Alateen, or to their family doctor. These people have experience in helping you to learn how to deal with an alcoholic parent and to sort out those worries you can solve and those you should leave to your parents.

When my parent drinks, I feel as if he doesn't care for me at all.

In part you feel this way because you are projecting your wish that he would not drink. Until they accept the fact that their parent has an illness, many teenagers say to themselves, "If my parent loved me he wouldn't drink."

Another reason you feel "unloved" by your parent is because of the inconsistency in your home. This inconsistency is one of the biggest problems a teenager has when living with an alcoholic parent or parents.

The effects of alcoholism cause the parent to show too much love one day and too little the next. One day your parent may praise you and the next day embarrass you. One day the alcoholic parent may sleep all day and the next day need all your attention. Under such conditions, it is very hard for the alcoholic to consistently show real parental feelings.

Emotional inconsistency is part of the pattern of alcoholism.

My mother is an alcoholic. My sister is on hard drugs. Can alcoholism in our home have driven her to taking drugs?

Studies have shown that there are more drug users among the children of alcoholic parents.

Your sister is in a sense copying your mother by using a chemical stimulus to satisfy her needs, and, like your mother, she is attempting to get satisfaction from sources other than real life.

Knowing all this may not help you too much in taking care of either your mother or your sister. You should see them as individual cases and help them as such. Most of all, don't assign automatic blame on your mother for your sister's problem. Try to find a drug-help center in your town and ask them what steps you should take to help your sister. Join Alateen and get help for yourself.

My father is an alcoholic. I have sworn not to drink. I take pot instead. My father is furious that I smoke pot. Isn't a joint safer than alcohol?

The difference between an occasional drink and an occasional joint is that you know exactly what is in a bottle of alcohol and that it is a legal drug.

A bottle of alcohol is labeled under government regulations with all of its ingredients.

The grass that comes from Mexico is different than grass from Asia or grass grown in the United States. Therefore, you are at the mercy of the one who sells or gives you the joint. Very often the seller or someone who gives you a joint has no way of knowing what strength or what type of grass is offered.

My mother is an alcoholic. My father travels. We never have enough food at home or proper meals. How can we help ourselves while my father is on the road?

Ask your father to give you the food money whenever he is on a trip and to let you talk to your physician about a proper diet suited to your life style. If for some reason this is not practical, speak to your school nurse. When your mother is sober, you should let her know that you need her and that her drinking is affecting your health.

Once you have a proper diet from your doctor or school nurse, you might find the "quick and easy" type recipes found in your library's cook book section fun to prepare.

If you have any specific questions on food, diet, or budgeting, write to the Office of Information, United States Department of Agriculture, Washington, D.C. 20250. Most booklets from the Department of Agriculture are free.

Both my parents are alcoholics. Every time they begin to drink, I eat anything I can get my hands on. When they don't drink, I am just as tense and nibble continually. Wouldn't I benefit from pills that control the appetite?

If you have a weight problem, consult a physician. For instance, you may have a low metabolism or an underactive thyroid gland. Be cautious of any drugs put on the market promising to kill your appetite. Many youngsters end up in the hospital because they innocently take drugs which do not agree with their physical makeup.

If you have a weight problem and a compulsive overeating habit, join Overeaters Anonymous. With the help and support of others who have the same problem, you can learn to express and handle your feelings and live with a compulsive eating disease.

I have heard it said that sometimes a teenager feels guilty because one of his parents drinks. Why should a teenager feel guilty if his parent drinks?

A teenager who lives with an alcoholic parent should not feel guilty because of his parent's drinking.

Sometimes teenagers in this situation may wonder if their behavior and their relationship with that parent may be driving him to drink.

Every family has problems and differences. A son or daughter may be dating someone whom his or her parents do not approve of. A teenager may have taken up a lifestyle which goes against the family traditions. The teenager may mistakenly think these problems are driving the parent to drink. But it is not the problems and differences within the family that are driving the parent to drink. It is alcoholism itself that has weakened his or her parent's ability to handle day-to-day family stress.

Couldn't some of these problems and emotions, such as not feeling loved, overeating, feeling guilty and nervous, occur in nonalcoholic families too?

Absolutely. Alcoholics are by no means the only people with problems. Extreme poverty, a father who works too hard and ignores the family, or any other serious kind of personality conflicts within the family may easily cause problems.

If you feel you do have a problem, whatever your problem may stem from—alcoholism in the home or other stresses—it pays at some point, while you are still young, to make the effort to deal with that problem.

What is most important in family life?

A family exists to help its members. A family should provide an atmosphere where each individual can mature and thrive. A family should be a foundation from which a teenager can test himself and grow in the outside world.

Are alcoholic parents at all interested in hearing how their children feel about family problems?

Definitely. Many teenagers avoid discussion with their parents, even when the alcoholic parent is not drinking, because they are afraid of a difference of opinion. If you talk sensibly about how you feel about your family, sticking to facts rather than criticizing, your parents might appreciate your feelings.

7

Your responsibility to yourself and to your family

My mother is an alcoholic. We don't have a father. I am the eldest of three children. Every time my mother passes out, I have to cancel dates and miss school because I end up not only nursing her but also taking care of my brother and sister. What can I do to help myself in a situation like this?

When your mother passes out, check to make sure she is breathing normally, and leave her, whenever possible, in the exact spot where she passed out. When she comes to, her unusual position, not being on the sofa or in bed comfortably covered, will perhaps jar her into realizing what she is doing to herself.

While your mother is incapacitated, you should do as few of her chores as possible. If you stay home from school to take over her job, you will be allowing her to continue this pattern. This is called "enabling." If your mother works outside the home, she may ask you to call the office for her when she doesn't feel well. By insisting that she do this, you will *not* be enabling, and may help her to see her problem from a different perspective.

Many a mother has pulled herself together because her family or a younger child needed her. If a mother is made to feel that her chores, her way of parenting, even her cooking can be replaced, she will continue to drink. When your mother is sober, you should tell her what it is like for you when she drinks, without criticising or insulting her. She may never have thought about what it is like for a son or daughter to stay home from school, or to have to cope with a mother's household chores. She may not know that you miss her when she passes out.

If your talking doesn't help, and your mother's alcoholism progresses, do not hesitate to go to Alateen or seek advice from family service, a school counselor, or a teenage walk-in center. The counselor you talk to may be able to supply your family with a part-time professional housekeeper to help you manage your home.

Whenever my mother is not intoxicated, she expects my brother and me to do all the cleaning. If we do not do a good job, she hits us. What can we do to make her stop being so finicky?

Your mother may be a perfectionist who is, when not drinking, projecting her frustrated, unhappy, miserable feelings on to you.

Is it at all possible for you to talk to your mother and make her aware that because of school you can devote only one or two hours a day to housework? Frequently the only solution is a schedule. The weekly schedule might include everything from "study for history exam" to "drama club" or "swim at the Y." You may find that once your mother knows you are not wasting time while not doing the housework, she will be more tolerant toward your work. Should your mother not be receptive to your needs, then her problem is one you cannot be expected to cope with. Many teenagers suffer from physical abuse by a parent or parents. You should seek help from a family service, a teenage walk-in center, or your clergyperson.

Both my parents are alcoholics. A counselor has been working with me and has told me I should help my par-

ents in the house. **What is the use of straightening up the house if one of my parents gets drunk and messes everything up again?**

You also live in the house. Should an alcoholic mess up the house after you cleaned it, it is very understandable that you would be most annoyed. However, once you decide to straighten up the house, do not use as an excuse "maybe my father will come home drunk." Simple everyday attitudes, like finishing what we start, get us into good work habits for the time we will be living on our own and holding down a job.

My father died when I was six years old, and my mother remarried quickly. My mother and stepfather are both heavy drinkers. When my stepfather drinks he makes sexual demands on me. When I complain to my mother, she slaps me and says I am imagining the whole thing. What can I do?

It is important that you immediately seek professional help. Your school nurse, your physician, school counselor, or such organizations as Women Against Rape, your local mental health clinic, or family counseling service and hotlines should all be able to aid you. Should you not feel comfortable with the first person you approach then seek someone else to talk to. The goal is to find someone who will not only believe you and understand the terror but also aid you in rebuilding your life.

You might like to know that most agencies today encourage family counseling as well as marital and individual counseling. The aim is to keep the family unit intact, learn to cope with stress, and deal with punitive reaction constructively. The intent is to rebuild the family and avoid any loss of jobs and standing in the community.

Your parents have tremendous stress they can't seem to cope with. Probably as children they themselves had poor parenting and, in a sense, are still like children today.

While alcohol complicates problems and lowers inhibitions, you should note that incest is not automatically related to drinking problems. The incidence of incest among families of alcoholics is no greater than among other families.

My mother is an alcoholic. I work very hard at home trying to help. I think one of the reasons I work so hard is that I want to be appreciated. But I do not get any consideration from my family. How can I get my family to appreciate me more?

Teenagers who work hard to help their parents by cooking, cleaning, and baby-sitting feel sometimes unappreciated not only by their parents but also by their brothers and sisters. Those who feel unappreciated owe it to themselves to find out why they feel this way.

The first knowledge we have of a relationship with a man or a woman is gained from our experiences at home. If you let the unpleasant feelings mature between you and your family, you will not only miss the experience of a happy family relationship, but it may also color your attitude toward all people for the rest of your life. For instance, if a girl feels her brother is more appreciated than she is, she may compete and fight more than is normal with her brother. When this girl gets married or has a job, she could unconsciously act the same way with her husband and with the men on the job. It can affect both her marriage and her job.

Parents do, without a doubt, sometimes appreciate one child more than another. If a mother's eldest son was born during a time she was trouble free, it may draw her closer to this son than to the rest of her children. In her eyes, any chores this son does are a perfect job. If the second youngest child is the brightest in her class, the parents are naturally going to talk a lot about her school work and the great help she is at home. This may make her brothers and sisters feel jealous.

Jealousy is often the cause of the "I am unappreciated" syndrome. Jealousy can do much to stifle an individual's character and personality development or may keep that person from being able to express appreciation for what is done for him or her. A jealous person is too busy competing with others to develop his or her own individuality. That person is never satisfied, always feels unappreciated, and is always looking for proof to justify the feeling of being the unwanted, unloved, and unappreciated child in the family.

If these are some of the reasons you feel unappreciated, they should not stop you from developing your own capabilities. Anyone who suffers from such feelings should try and discuss it with their parents when they are sober. Sometimes family annoyances are so deeply rooted that they cannot be settled within the family. Some cases go so far that it is no longer possible for members of the family to sit down and communicate. In such cases seek the friendship and support you can get from Alateen or professional help.

Keep in mind that while parents may not appreciate one child enough, worry more about another, or find it easier to confide in a third child, they do in most cases— even though they may not be able to express it well—love all of their children. One mother explained her love this way: "My children are like my own ten fingers. If I were to lose one, I would miss that finger terribly even though I would have nine others left." Wouldn't you, too?

8

It's your school life and future

My mother's alcoholism exhausts me and keeps me from studying. What can I do?

First of all, join Alateen. There you will find teenagers who face similar problems. You will be able to share your feelings and make new friends.

Try to get your father (or if you have no father, a professional person) to take an interest in your problem. Your father may never have realized that your mother is so demanding and noisy when you are with her that you cannot get your homework done. He may not know that, because of her alcoholism, she has forgotten notices, meetings, and conferences with your school or has embarrassed you by showing up at school intoxicated.

Your father may never have been aware that your mother, like so many alcoholics, may criticize whatever you do so much that she may have undermined your self-confidence and capability to do school work.

Not all learning problems can be automatically blamed on alcoholism. Sometimes students who do not wish to study for other reasons use alcoholism in the home as an excuse for not doing their work.

How can students who do poorly in school because of alcoholism in the home help themselves?

In the files of a public school counselor is the case history of Kenneth, a boy who was determined to do something about his predicament.

Fifteen-year-old Kenneth knew that he wanted to be a carpenter. He had looked into the requirements and realized that he would need special training. Kenneth was doing so badly in school that he was seriously thinking of dropping out; but first, he decided, he would discuss it with his school counselor. The counselor arranged to have Kenneth tested. Kenneth showed good ability in his tests. However, upon further questioning, the counselor learned that Kenneth had trouble concentrating because he felt worried and was restless and tired most of the time. The counselor questioned Kenneth about his study schedule at home. Kenneth explained that he could not keep a study schedule. His mother was an alcoholic. His father traveled a lot, so she drank mostly in the evening when she was alone.

Kenneth usually went to bed at eleven. His mother would come and wake him at one in the morning, not realizing the time, and say, "I am lonely, why don't you talk to me?" His mother had been placed in a hospital several times. It always upset Kenneth to see the ambulance arrive. While his mother was in the hospital, he had to do many time-consuming chores which left him too tired for his homework. Kenneth concluded, "Counseling can't change my home life, and how your testing can help someone like me, is beyond me."

The counselor had Kenneth's father come to school to see what arrangements could be made for Kenneth to sleep at a friend's house whenever his mother drank. What interested the counselor was that Kenneth told her he could not concentrate even when he tried to study in school, at a friend's house, or at the library. The counselor told Kenneth that it is understandable a life such as his would make a teenager angry and keep him from studying. She went on to tell him this type of anger may frequently be against oneself, and it might, in part, be anger that has nothing to do with the family.

Any teenager may be upset that he does not achieve his high expectations in school. This may include not only grades but also popularity, athletic achievements, and coping with personal problems. That pretty girl in algebra class does not even know you are alive. Or, that handsome boy in intermediate Spanish does not even nod at you.

Kenneth asked, "But what about the feeling of frustration and anger that you can't pinpoint?" He said this was how he felt different from the other students. He could understand why he was upset when his social life was bad or his mother drank; but he also said he had this upset feeling even when his mother was not drinking, and all was well in school. His mind would wander to the last time his mother drank, or he would worry if she might drink again. Then one day, while discussing this feeling with his counselor, he made an admission to himself which opened a whole new outlook on the problem. Kenneth, because he loved his parents, wanted things to be right at home. Since he could not make them right, he felt frustrated and angry within himself. This was, in part, why he could not concentrate. Once he understood where his restlessness came from, he had a certain amount of relief.

The counselor told Kenneth many teenagers from nonalcoholic homes feel a similar restlessness. There are teenagers whose parents want to get divorced, or who have a parent in debt or continually in court. They feel frustrated, too, that they cannot solve their parents' problems. Unfortunately, there are some problems that never can be solved, and it is a waste of energy to worry over them. The only thing a teenager can do is recognize those problems that do not belong to him and try not to worry about them.

It is a big and difficult job, but it can be achieved. At

first Kenneth thought he could never do it. But he found the more he practiced it, the more it helped him.

Alateen opens all meetings with this prayer:

God grant me the serenity
To accept the things I cannot change,
Courage to change the things I can,
And wisdom to know the difference.

Kenneth might encourage his mother not to drink by letting her know that chronic drinking is a disease, and he could not solve her drinking problem for her. Nor would it help him or his mother to worry when she might have to go to the hospital.

Worrying can be a form of procrastination. You sit down to study, but you let your mind dwell on other things: "If Mom didn't drink, we would have a less banged-up home." Yet, when you go to an interesting movie, your mind does not wander because you want to enjoy yourself.

Kenneth's counselor told him that when he found it hard to concentrate, he should phone a friend he could trust and talk out his feelings. Talking about frustrations and fears helps to overcome helpless and angry feelings. This is why talking out your feelings with a trusted person is so helpful.

Do all children of alcoholics have problems in school?

No. As contradictory as it may seem, many students who have alcoholic parents, because of what they have experienced at home, are often more self-sufficient and stand up better to the challenge in school than their colleagues. Because an alcoholic parent is a demanding parent, his son or daughter frequently turns out to be an above-average student.

9

Friends and dating

Should I tell my friends my mother is an alcoholic before I bring them home?

If you are truly embarrassed by your mother's drinking, maybe you should phone home before you bring a friend over. If your mother sounds bad on the phone, and you do not choose to tell your friends about the alcoholism at home, you can explain to your friend that your mother is sick today.

Many teenagers today want to confide in their friends. They say it is easier today than ever before to explain alcoholism to other teenagers because the hallmark of the modern teenager is compassion and a concern for their fellow human beings.

Other teenagers of alcoholic parents feel they can bring their friends home without any explanations. It does not matter to them if their friends see their parent intoxicated once in a while. They feel it is not necessary to share the information that they live with an alcoholic parent. The friend's natural reaction will probably be that it happens only occasionally.

Most of these boys and girls generally think that if their friends in school have not had experience with alcoholism, and they start to tell them about it, their friends will not know how to handle the information. While meaning well, friends might come up to them frequently and ask, "How are things at home?" as if he or she expected a sob story from them every other day.

My father is an alcoholic. One night I had a rough time at home. Foolishly I confided my problems to one of the boys in school who promptly burst out laughing and yelled, "Oh, boy, your old man gets stoned!" What can make a teenager act so unkindly?

People sometimes react with laughter when they don't know how to handle a situation or when they are presented with familiar facts in an unfamiliar environment. Most youngsters giggle at anything unfamiliar, such as the idea of an intoxicated parent, when they are age ten, eleven, or twelve. The older we get, the better we can accept unfamiliar facts. By the time we are thirteen or fourteen, we are capable of "putting our feet in someone else's shoes."

Only an insecure thirteen- or fourteen-year-old teenager would be prompted to make an unkind remark. Making fun of someone else makes the insecure person feel as if he or she is super OK.

A helpful guideline is to remember that when we are upset we cannot explain things very well. That is the time we want to confide in a true and trustworthy friend—or in someone who has a similar situation at home.

I have a few good friends who have no experience with alcoholism at home. I feel guilty when I explain to them the situation at home. How can I confide in my close friends?

As long as you explain your parent's condition as an illness, but do not get personal about their actions (such as how they talk or walk), there is no reason to feel guilty about what you confide in a friend.

My mother is an alcoholic. I can remember when, as a little kid, mothers didn't let their children play at my

house because they didn't trust my home. Today, I am the one who is too embarrassed to let the kids see what state my mother is in. How can I ever make friends?

The opportunities for teenagers of alcoholic parents to meet new people are no different from those for any other teenager. When you were little you met children at the playground or in front of the house where the other mothers could see and supervise what was going on. But today you are a teenager, and as a teenager your opportunities to meet friends are almost all outside your home. You meet people in such places as school, clubs, churches, synagogues, or where you have a job. When you meet someone for the first time in school, at that moment, the boy or girl you are talking to cannot see your father, mother, sister, brother, or your furniture, or your house. By the time you bring your friend home, the impression of you will already be formed. In your mind, as you talk to a fellow teenager, you may think of your home environment and feel awkward and uncomfortable. Our frame of mind can often keep us from acting the warm and considerate persons we really are. You may feel uncomfortable because you remember when, as a young child, mothers did not want their children to play with you. This experience is over and should not stop you from making friends today.

Popularity is not solely determined by the type of parents you have. There are plenty of youngsters who have pleasant parents but are unpopular because they are shy, insecure, or hesitant in reaching for others. A likable person is someone who is sincere, has unique ideas, is considerate, and is unselfish.

Isn't it true that it is hard to have really close friends if you cannot bring a friend home?

Good friends will understand the situation in your house and why you don't bring them to your home. They themselves may not want to go to your home when your parent is drinking. This is no reason to break up good friendships. You can reciprocate any friend's hospitality in other ways, such as helping him or her to get chores done quickly, helping with the dishes if you are invited for a meal, and just by being a sincere friend.

Remember, your friends probably want friends as much as you do.

My father is an alcoholic who has stopped drinking. He is still very rigid and tense. The slightest noise upsets him. I literally cannot bring friends home. I would like to give a party at my house. How can I get my father to change?

With participation in Alcoholics Anonymous, your father will find help and support. He will probably need to make big changes in his life to relax and enjoy his sobriety.

You may have fun outside the home by going bowling or skating with your friends. Or perhaps you are lucky enough to have a relative or a good friend who would let you give a party in their home. People who offer their home should be given the following courtesy:

(1) Ask your hosts how many people you may invite. Every homeowner knows, from past experience, how many people are comfortable in the home.

(2) Discuss in great detail what kind of a party it will be—a barbecue, dancing, etc. This way your hosts will not surprise you the night of the party by saying, "All those records? We thought you were just going to have one guitar. The neighbors will never stand for all that noise."

(3) Ask your hosts whether they or someone else will be home the night of the party. After all, it is not your home, and if something goes wrong, you are better off having an adult around to take the responsibility. An adult can handle anyone trying to crash your party or any impulsive guests.

(4) Offer to pay for the refreshments.

(5) Offer to clean up after the party.

(6) The next day phone or write a thank you note. It might be a nice gesture to buy a little gift to thank them for the use of their home.

My father disapproves of the gang I hang around with. I disapprove of his drinking. Do I have a right to tell him to mind his own business?

Even though your father is an alcoholic, he is your parent and does worry about you. Parents worry about gangs because who you select as friends can mean life or death. If your crowd believes in antisocial acts such as fast driving or stealing, or going to parties where drugs are used, even though you might not join in these activities, you could make yourself look guilty.

Teenagers who feel they want popularity will sometimes join a crowd. There is a form of security in a gang. In a gang, teenagers feel they belong. There is a leader to follow. Members will let all joiners feel they are welcome if the teenagers do what they want. Those who do not comply are left out. Before you join the gang, have a look at whether they're doing your type of thing. Those who look for nothing but a gang of friends are apt to have very few friends. They are so busy getting to know everyone that they have no time to get to know a few people well. If you are having problems breaking away from a gang, or have difficulties making friends on your own, join organized sports, a club at your local church, or group activities at your YMCA, YWCA, or your community center.

Perhaps alcoholism in the home can make a person too sensitive. I personally find that my feelings are easily hurt. What can I do to help myself?

The very experience of growing up, the hormonal changes in the body, and newly awakened interest in the opposite sex can make any teenager feel sensitive.

Naturally, any extreme problem, such as alcoholism, can make us even more sensitive and vulnerable. Should your alcoholic parent be of the same sex as you, it is doubly difficult for you to find an image to believe in and a role model to make you feel secure. Once you are aware of your need to have an image of your parent to be proud of, you can try to take those values you admire when your parent is sober. Should your parent's alcoholism have turned you off to such a degree that you cannot be objective even when she is sober, then seek out a counselor of your own sex to discuss your feelings.

My father is an alcoholic and always interferes in my dating. The trouble is that his rules for dating vary from day to day. What can I do?

Some parents have a hard time setting rules and make different rules every time their son or daughter goes out. Try to discuss the dating rules each night before you go out. It will prevent a lot of misunderstandings.

You may find that on the day your father insists that you "be home at 10 o'clock," something prompted him to be fearful. It may have been an article he read in the newspaper about a teenager getting killed in a car accident. You might, in fact, ask him why he wants you home earlier this time. His explanation may be reasonable. Whatever the reason, and no matter how unpleasantly he expresses it, he is showing concern about you.

Try to set sensible dating standards for yourself. Should you not be able to get the kind of information you want from your family, pick out a family you admire and ask the teenager in that family about the standards or rules for dating. Or, if you do not know such a family, do not hesitate to discuss your dating with a counselor at a teenage walk-in center, at a teenage coffeehouse, or with a favorite clergyperson.

I am a sixteen-year-old girl who is happy to get out of the house whenever I can. Sometimes when I date, I stay

out all night. My mother then calls me names. What right does my mother, as an alcoholic, have to think poorly of me?

Obviously, your mother is worried about where you spend your nights. She may suspect you are engaged in sexual activity she feels is harmful to you.

Your mother may be ill, but she is still a parent. When your mother is sober, discuss with her what dating was like in her day and how she feels about dating today. Once you discuss dating with your mother, you might find her attitude changing more to your point of view. You might also find that some of her questions are valid and that you have been using her alcoholism as an excuse to avoid facing criticism.

What are some of the concerns my mother may have?

Primarily, parents are concerned about your attitude toward sex. Parents feel sex is a tremendous responsibility for a teenage girl because you can get tied down with an unexpected pregnancy. If you do not have a partner who is steady only with you, and who has been checked out by a doctor, there is a chance that you may get venereal disease. Your mother may be worried about how much your partner considers your feelings. All those endearing words he says are a responsibility. She may wonder about your own promises of love and if it may lead to an unwanted marriage.

My father is an alcoholic. I am eighteen and want to get married. Both my parents say I am too young. In our state, you do not need permission to get married when you are eighteen, so I think I will just go ahead without my parents' blessings.

Deep down, your parents know that their home has been a chaotic one. They may not know why their home has been chaotic, but are concerned about what their home has done to you and whether you are ready for marriage.

Sometimes boys and girls are discouraged by the chaos at home. They hope that marriage will solve their problems. Marriage makes them feel someone cares and gives them the hope of having a trouble-free home of their own.

Too often, when we have not worked out the confusion and the unhappiness we saw at home, we not only bring our troubles into our marriage but also find it difficult to cope with the new responsibilities marriage has brought us.

If your parents do not approve of your upcoming marriage, and you do not see eye to eye with your parents, at least talk to a marriage counselor or to a clergyperson you have confidence in to get another, hopefully objective, viewpoint.

Marriage is a highly personal matter. Couldn't counseling only destroy the romance and love between two people?

Counseling will only strengthen and mature your love. A counselor will give you the confidence to know you are marrying for the right reasons.

Give a case history of how alcoholism in the home affected a teenager's decision to marry.

There are many, many case histories, and each one is different. The following is one of these case histories:

"I wish somebody had talked to me about dating when I was fifteen or had told me to read up on dating. My mother was an alcoholic, and my father had walked out on us. I could not stand to see my mother drink. When things were bad at home, I would run out with the first date available. Anything to get out. If any young person were to ask me today what to do when things are bad at home, I would say, 'Don't go out on a date for the sake of a date. Go to old friends to whom you can talk, join

Alateen, or stay overnight with a family who knows your situation at home.'

"I didn't. One day I met a man fifteen years older than I. He was divorced, and he knew what life was about. I admired him. He was for me what I had always wanted— a father. He gave me the affection and admiration I didn't get at home. He gave me the advice I didn't get at home.

"My mother did not approve of him. She said he was too old for me. But there was a wonderful feeling in knowing someone was always ready to go out with me. When I think back, I didn't really love him. I just did not want to be bothered to look for other people to date. It was the first time in my life that I had a shoulder to cry on, and I thought that was enough. We got married when I was seventeen; and, now, at eighteen, I have a baby. There is not enough money because he has to pay alimony to his first wife and child. I have to work as a waitress at night to make ends meet. There does not seem to be time or money for going out even to a movie. On Sunday I am alone because he goes to visit his other child. Now that we are married, I don't enjoy his know-it-all attitude which made me feel so secure before we were married. I wish I had someone close to my age who understands how I think.

"I feel that my friends are having fun dancing, traveling, studying, or working exciting jobs or buying pretty clothes while I am stuck at home. I feel that my future has been shortchanged."

My mother is an alcoholic. I got into trouble because my mother encouraged me to start dating at the age of twelve. What caused her to get me to date so young?

Your mother may have felt badly that you could not have friends to your house because of her drinking. Dating may have made your mother feel as if you had belonged to a group and, in general, were accepted by society.

I am a sixteen-year-old girl. When my first date came to my house to pick me up, my father, who was drunk, fell down the front stairs. When we tried to help him up, he became abusive. What can girls in this situation do when their dates expect to pick them up at home?

When a boy asks you out for the first time and your alcoholic parent is drinking, offer to meet him elsewhere. If your alcoholic parent begins to drink a few hours before you expect your date, you can avoid the problem by phoning your date at his home to say your plans have changed, and ask him if he would mind meeting you elsewhere. It can be a girlfriend's house, a relative's house, or a reputable place in the center of the town. Your date may ask you why he cannot come to your house. Should you feel at this point that you don't want to confide in him, you can make up a plausible excuse, such as, "I am at my girlfriend's house because she asked me to help her baby-sit for her younger sister until you come." Those teenage girls who meet their date away from home should realize that their parents might feel worried about who their date is and where they are meeting him. Remember, even though a parent is an alcoholic, she feels responsible for you. It is understandable that you may not always like the manner in which your parent's illness causes her to show parental concern, but concern it is. It is wise to tell your parents, or at least your sober parent, who your date is, where you are going, and why they shouldn't worry. "We are not driving" or "He is an excellent driver" or "You know that I am very careful" are comments that may lessen their fears.

If your parents do have objections, however, you must think them over carefully. Let your parents feel that you want them to meet your date. You might say, "As soon as you stop your drinking, I'll bring him home." Hopefully, such comments will motivate your parent to stop drinking. Whatever you do, do not use the fact that you are meeting your dates on the outside as a weapon to criticize your parents. You can make your parents aware that the reason you don't bring friends home is not because you are not proud of your parents, but because alcoholism is a disease that does not show them in their true light.

Both my parents are alcoholics. I am dating a girl I really like. I am afraid if I tell her my parents drink, she may lose interest in me. Should I keep dating her without telling her about my parents?

It is not necessary to tell a girl you take out the first or second time about your problems at home. But if you are going "steady," exchanging intimate information is part of being close to each other.

It is questionable how worthwhile a person your girlfriend is if she cannot accept the fact that you have two ill parents.

One teenager told how he was very shy about telling his new girlfriend about the alcoholism at home. When he finally started to tell her, she interrupted him. Instead, she poured her heart out how her parents, who do not drink, either fight or do not talk at all to each other and were on the verge of a divorce. Her problem had nothing to do with alcoholism but seemed just as hard to her. She was glad to have a boyfriend who could understand her. Being an understanding person and knowing how to explain your life at home will help you when dating.

10

Can alcoholism be cured?

How can alcoholism be cured?
As far as we know, the only way an alcoholic can return to normal life is by giving up alcohol completely. Alcoholics react differently to alcohol than do other people. Many times they need to seek help to stop drinking.

I have heard that when alcoholics give up drinking they experience withdrawal syndromes. What is meant by withdrawal syndromes?
Withdrawal syndromes are reactions that occur when alcohol is taken away from a person who is accustomed to regular use of alcohol.
It is as if the brain had a thermostat which was set higher because it was expecting to be slowed down by alcohol. Once the brain has become adapted to regular use of alcohol, a big rebound occurs when it is taken away. Without the alcohol, all the brain functions increase for a period of time until the thermostat readjusts.

How do these withdrawal syndromes appear?
In mild cases, withdrawal syndromes cause tremors or shaking of the hands. If a person who has been drinking, and who has a long drinking history behind him or her, has a tremor in the morning, it can be relieved by a drink or two; but this is a sign of alcoholism.

The withdrawal syndromes can also result in the person seeing things that aren't there (hallucinations), in convulsions which are just like epileptic seizures, and, in the most serious cases, in delirium tremens (DT s).

What happens when an alcoholic has DT s?

This is the most serious type of withdrawal reaction. It usually starts about three days after drinking has ceased. It may start with a convulsion. The alcoholic begins hearing, feeling, and seeing things that aren't there. The alcoholic is disoriented and doesn't know where he is or what is happening. He may be very frightened. He has a rapid pulse count, profuse sweating, and a high fever. The alcoholic should be in the hospital. If a doctor can't be found, the police will help to get him to the hospital.

What are convulsions?

A convulsion is a "mass discharge" of signals from the overactive brain. The person loses consciousness, the body undergoes a rhythmical series of muscular contractions, the eyes may turn to one side. Then the body stiffens to a very rigid position with all the muscles contracted, and breathing stops. After this, there is a relaxation of the muscles and deep breathing. Within a short time the person may awaken and will not remember what happened. The convulsion may repeat, or there may be only one. Convulsions usually occur between twelve and twenty-four hours after drinking has ceased and do not usually recur.

What can one do to help the alcoholic when he or she has a convulsion?

Keep the person's head turned to the side, and keep your fingers away from her mouth. Otherwise, beyond loosening the collar and belt and being sure that the alcoholic doesn't hurt herself by moving her arms and legs, one should not interfere with her at this time. The alcoholic will get over the convulsion.

What are some steps that can be taken to help an alcoholic parent?

The first and most important step is for the whole family to recognize that the parent is ill and has lost control of his use of alcohol.

The second step is for the alcoholic to want to do something about the disease. While the alcoholic is the only one who can conquer the dependency on alcohol, there are hospitals, clinics, social and religious agencies, and groups such as Alcoholics Anonymous ready and equipped to give an experienced hand. The alcoholic will usually seek out these agencies once he realizes this is an illness. The family members have to realize that their encouragement while the alcoholic is seeking help can aid the person in conquering his dependency on alcohol.

The earlier a family recognizes an alcoholic in their midst, the easier it will be for them to cope with the disease and perhaps make the alcoholic aware that there is hope.

My father is an alcoholic. He became furious when I told him to seek help. Why can't I get through to him?

Your father misunderstood what you were trying to tell him. Your father, at this point, is still afraid of the future. He worries about how he could live without alcohol. He still does not have enough insight into his illness to ask himself why he drinks and to face the fact that he is addicted to alcohol.

If the family does not succeed in making the alcoholic realize he or she is ill, should a son or daughter seek someone outside the family to talk to the alcoholic?

It might help, provided the person you seek out has knowledge of alcoholism. If you get someone who warns the alcoholic with "Pull yourself together" or "Aren't you ashamed of yourself?" more damage than good can be done.

Do not be upset if the first person you go to for help does not understand your problem at home. They may be good friends and wonderful people, but they may not have had experience in helping alcoholics. Do not give up. Go talk to your family doctor, or a counselor at school. Perhaps your clergyperson has had experience with alcoholism.

What can friends, clergy, or a doctor tell the alcoholic that the family has not told him already?

Friends, clergy, and doctors are all in a position to motivate the alcoholic to seek help.

A family has to live with the alcoholic's arguments. The alcoholic may be so used to the family's urgings that he may not pay attention to them anymore. Certain family members may still be denying the illness. They may be covering up for the alcoholic or trying to change the situation.

When a friend speaks, the alcoholic cannot help but take note that the drinking has gone so far that even friends are concerned about him.

A doctor can give a medical diagnosis that the person is alcoholic and let him know that if he is willing to cooperate, a proper course of action can be prescribed.

Clergy can draw on the experience of dealing with other alcoholics in the parish. He or she might guide the alcoholic to a clinic or to Alcoholics Anonymous, or introduce him to a recovering alcoholic who would help him realize that there are others afflicted with this disease, and who are succeeding in recovering their health.

Does Alcoholics Anonymous have a religious affiliation?

Many people mistakenly think that A.A. is run by a religious group. Alcoholics Anonymous is not allied with any sect, denomination, political organization, or institution.

Is Alcoholics Anonymous expensive?

There are no fees or dues. A basket is passed at each meeting, but nobody looks to see if everyone gives or how much one gives.

What exactly does Alcoholics Anonymous do?

Alcoholics Anonymous is a worldwide fellowship of men and women who help each other to maintain sobriety and who offer to share their recovery experience freely with others who may have a drinking problem. At each meeting alcoholics tell how they managed to stop drinking and how long it has been since they last had a drink.

Alcoholics Anonymous in Your Community, distributed by A.A. publications, describes A.A. as a "Method of treating alcoholism in which members act as therapists to each other, sharing with each other a large body of similar experiences in suffering and recovering from alcoholism."

When an alcoholic comes to A.A. and says he or she would like to try to stop drinking, the alcoholic is introduced to a "sponsor." The alcoholic may phone the sponsor who is a fellow alcoholic whenever—no matter what time of day or night—the urge to drink cannot be controlled.

Some are afraid to join Alcoholics Anonymous because they fear they will "slip" and start to drink and that their cohorts might lose confidence in them. People in A.A. never lose confidence or give up. Alcoholics in A.A. whose drinking has been arrested understand the slips, the good and the bad moods, because they have experienced them, too.

The program includes "Twelve suggested Steps" to help the alcoholic maintain sobriety. The most important Step is the first one: "We admitted we were powerless over alcohol—that our lives had become unmanageable." *

---

* *Alcoholics Anonymous* published by A.A. World Services, New York, N.Y. Available through Hazelden Educational Materials.

Alcoholics Anonymous has excellent literature which explains in great detail how the program helps the alcoholic. Once you receive this literature, the other members in your immediate family might also be interested in reading it. After seeing it, the one who needs A.A. might even be encouraged to seek help.

Some of the information comes in comic book form. The comics "What Happened to Joe and His Drinking Problem" and "It Happened to Alice" are especially good.

This literature is available at your local A.A. meetings. If you do not find A.A. listed in your local phone book and want to know which town near you has A.A., write to Alcoholics Anonymous, Box 459 Grand Central P.O., New York, N.Y. 10017.

Do teenagers ever visit A.A.?

Yes. You will feel welcomed at A.A. and might meet other teenagers who are in the same predicament as you. It is not unusual for teenagers to go to open Alcoholics Anonymous meetings to listen and to talk to the recovering alcoholics. Such a visit will give you hope that your parents, too, can regain their health, and, by listening to the alcoholics present, you will gain insight into their suffering.

What do they do at the closed meetings?

The same as at the opening meetings—but new members sometimes feel freer to work out their problems when they are among fellow alcoholics only.

Do women also attend Alcoholics Anonymous?

Yes. A.A. is for both men and women. Women usually have a female sponsor; men, a male.

What type of a person is a sponsor?

A sponsor is a fellow citizen in your town who has a drinking problem similar to that of your parent. She has managed to arrest the drinking by following the A.A. program. You will find that A.A. has many active, honored, and talented citizens in your town. What impresses and encourages the new A.A. members is how the sponsors, who once had the same problem as the new members, now look healthy, are full of pep and zest, and appear happy.

Is A.A. the only source of help available to the alcoholic?

There are many other sources of help. Many hospitals and clinics have facilities and medical aid available to the alcoholic. Most states today have extensive alcoholism programs set up in conjunction with their state university or with their public health, mental health, or social welfare departments.

The A.A. program is so successful because it is a self-help group. The A.A. method has proven so full of merit that many hospitals accepting alcoholic patients hold A.A. meetings within their medical complex.

How are alcoholics treated at a clinic or hospital?

The clinic takes the drinking history of the patient: when and how he started to drink, how long he has been drinking heavily, the pattern of drinking, and his life history in general. The clinic finds out what past stresses he experienced in school, in his career, with parents and his present family, and with the opposite sex.

The clinic may choose to interview a relative to get a wider perspective and may encourage and offer therapy to the whole family so that they can work out their own hurt that comes from living with an alcoholic.

The case will be discussed at a staff meeting by those who interviewed the alcoholic so that the extent of the drinking problem may be assessed and the best course of action may be decided on.

It may be decided to keep the person hospitalized to help him through withdrawal symptoms and regain physical health. They may have the alcoholic attend group therapy as well as undergo individual therapy during the hospital stay. Clinics do have, in most instances, outpatient follow-up programs.

Is there a central agency where I can find out about all the facilities in our town for alcoholics?
Phone your "Alcoholism Information Center" listed in your phone book or call a medical facility.

11

When a parent stops drinking

What motivates an alcoholic finally to stop drinking?
The alcoholic's own realization that her addiction can be helped if she has the honest desire to stop drinking.

My father is an alcoholic who is trying to stop drinking. He is so ill-tempered that I think life was easier while he was drinking. What is making him so moody and difficult?
The convalescing period is frequently a very long period and a very difficult time for the alcoholic. Your father is still experiencing tensions and depressions, among other things. Attending A.A. meetings will help your father greatly with these problems.

What, in general, is involved in an alcoholic's recovery period?
An alcoholic's recovery consists generally of four phases. The first, as we have already mentioned, is the alcoholic's realization that he can be helped. The alcoholic admits to himself that he has a problem with alcohol and surrenders to it. During this first stage, the alcoholic may gain hope by meeting recovering alcoholics who are normal and happy. Help can also come through an understanding clergyperson or psychiatrist.

During this period the alcoholic will start eating regularly, and in some cases he will go to the doctor to get a thorough checkup. He may need vitamins after many years of poor eating, or some of the internal organs may have been affected by the heavy drinking and may need treatment.

In the second phase, the alcoholic begins to share life with the family and leave the isolation which he has experienced. He begins to see that he drank to cope with feelings of hopelessness and sense of failure, for example.

As time goes on, the alcoholic will enter the third phase which starts when he begins to get to know himself better. The alcoholic begins to have a new awareness of "pressure points" or the kind of thinking and emotional reactions which have pressured him to use the bottle. As the therapy continues, he will grow emotionally, take stress better, and desire the escape of alcohol less and less. The third step is really the core of the recovery process.

In the final stage, the alcoholic gains confidence in his ability to work; he wants to help others with their problem of alcoholism and is willing to continue getting therapy or counseling when the desire to drink arises.

How long does the convalescing period take?

Each alcoholic needs a different amount of time. The whole convalescing period can take anywhere from one month to two years.

How does one know when the alcoholic is rehabilitated?

Alcoholics say that when they feel sobriety is preferable to their old life, they are on the way to a safe recovery.

My mother is an alcoholic. She did not touch a drink for two years, and we all felt she had complete insight into her alcoholism. One day, for no reason in particular,

she went back to drinking. How can such behavior be explained?

As in any disease, relapses may occur. Giving up their therapy too soon or not attending A.A. meetings can be a mistake. Gradually, as your mother continues with her therapy, she will realize that drinking will not solve her problems, and her bouts should become fewer.

Is there any way a family can recognize an alcoholic's anxieties?

Yes. Signs of anxieties are increased smoking of cigarettes, cigars, or pipes; walking up and down; clenching of a fist; or extreme silences or talkativeness.

What can the family do to alleviate an alcoholic's anxieties?

You should show faith in the ability of the alcoholic parent whenever possible. Comments like "Mom I am so glad you haven't had a drink in six months" will make it all worthwhile to her. If an alcoholic father makes a good barbecue, or you appreciate that he took you to the ball game, let him know it. As long as the comments are sincere, they will be effective. Alcoholics are sensitive people and can see through a compliment for the sake of a compliment.

My father is an alcoholic who has not touched a drink in fifteen months. The fact that he does not drink does not make him any fairer to his children. For instance, one day he says we may use the family car, and the next day, for no reason whatsoever, he will not let us use his car. What makes some alcoholic parents so inconsistent even after they have stopped drinking?

A parent may continue or retain the pattern of inconsistency he had while actively drinking, even when he is no longer drinking. In such a situation, it is wise to take each permission to do something as an individual occasion, as the rule of the day, or even, the moment. Involvement in A.A. can help the parent a great deal with this inconsistent behavior.

12

Counseling for the teenager

What does counseling for the teenager involve?

The counselor listens to the teenager. The counselor is interested in what worries her, what the complaints are, what she has lived through. The counselor helps a person to vent thoughts and think through the best course of action.

A counselor may help you to understand you are not the reason for the excessive drinking in your home and help you to understand your own reaction to it. While the counselor will not tell you what to do, she may help you to understand the situation you live with, and offer guidelines and some course of action for coping with such a dilemma.

Where can a teenager obtain counseling?

Today, there are many services geared specifically to teenagers. First to be considered is Alateen, which consists of groups of teenagers who meet to discuss the problem of living with alcoholic parents.

Furthermore, many churches, community centers, teenage coffeehouses, and family service agencies sponsor teenage walk-in services. These walk-in services are prepared to deal with *all* kinds of problems, not just alcoholism.

Why is it called "teenage walk-in center"?

Because a teenager can walk in without an appointment and talk to a counselor about anything that he or she may be concerned with.

Who are the counselors?

The counselors are social workers who specifically understand a teenager's needs.

Are there other kids around when I talk to the counselor?

The counselor talks to you alone in a private room. In addition, some walk-in centers offer group rap sessions for those teenagers who enjoy it.

If I go to a walk-in center, will my parents be involved?

These centers do not phone your parents unless you want them to be involved. Sometimes these counselors can reach a parent when a son or daughter cannot. Experience has taught the counselors that even the most difficult, ill-tempered parents are not beyond help, but can be helped by a therapist who knows how to relate to them.

My parents are so impossible that no counselor can talk to them. What does the center do when parents are beyond help?

Not all family problems are solved easily. A teenager may come from a home where he simply cannot thrive because the environment does not meet his needs. The center will discuss with such families the advantages of boarding schools or the possibility that the teenager might live with a favorite relative.

If a case is very difficult, and the parents do not cooperate, the center may place a teenager with a "host," or foster family until the parents are able to resume their responsibilities. The center may discuss with the teenager whether he wants to leave home and refer him to a proper social agency which has the legal power to move him out of his home. Many times, the counselor involved works overtime to help.

What is a host family?

A host family is a family living in or near your community who is willing and able to offer their home on very short notice to a teenager who may need a place to stay for a night or two.

Both my parents drink. I hate it at home. I don't want to wait until some agency decides where I should go. As long as I can hitchhike, I can make my way.

Before you do anything, speak to a counselor you trust, find out what the laws are concerning minors in your state, and consider the alternatives to running away. A counselor will tell you how life can be made more tolerable at home or at least help you leave with an open door behind you in case you want to come back.

Many teenagers say that running away is the quickest and easiest solution to unpleasant family problems. The open road may look attractive, but many who have walked it have told stories of lives spent in fear. If they are underage and someone robs them or abuses them, they are afraid to call the police for fear they will be caught. This makes them easy prey for thieves and other criminals.

If you do get caught, you take a chance of being put in a detention center or a state institution. Some states have excellent institutions. However, if you are the one to approach a counselor, you can discuss with her what facilities are available without having a court decide where you should go.

Where can I find out whether there is a walk-in center in our town or any other counseling facility geared to teenagers?

Very often walk-in centers place posters in the schools. Phone your local "hot line." Look up family service, or youth service, in your local phone book. Ask your local newspaper, library, school counselor, clergyperson, physician, mental health association, or a teacher what services exist for those who want help.

What is a hot line?

A hot line is a telephone number a teenager can dial. The person who answers is a fellow teenager or a counselor who knows about the various facilities in the town. The person who answers the phone will give any immediate advice or comfort needed. Names of the callers are never asked.

What is family therapy?

Family therapy is a form of psychotherapy. All it means is that the family all gets together to discuss their thoughts, problems, and ideas with an objective counselor. The goal behind this is for family members to learn to relate and function better as a family.

Each family has its own way of doing things and reacting to life's problems. When an objective person is present, the family can learn to see its own strengths and weaknesses and learn as one unit how to help themselves. Parents often come out of these sessions with a better understanding of how alcoholism in the family has hurt their children. And the children gain insight into their parents' problems, what they, as children, can do to lessen the tension and strife at home.

Both my parents drink. I contacted family service, and I am seeing a counselor there. My older sister thinks it is disgusting that I tell my counselor about our family. My sister needs help as much as I do. How can I get her to come to a family service agency?

Your sister's feelings describe many teenagers' feelings. She may think her problems are unique, or that it is a sign of weakness to seek help. She may feel the group will judge her. Instead of showing compassion, she fears the agency or the professional giving guidance might only point out the faults and mistakes of the family members.

Your sister will have the courage to seek help once she sees it as a way to get more information about how to handle her life. Her story will be respected and will not invade the family privacy. No professional person can reveal confidential information for both ethical and legal reasons. For instance, no report may be automatically released to your parents.

The more you share your experience of seeking help with your sister, the less guarded she will be.

My father is an alcoholic. My mother says she knows all about counseling, but she won't let me go. How can I convince my mother to let me go to counseling or to Alateen?

On occasion, one will hear of cases where a teenager realizes his or her parent is sick and would like to seek help, but one or both parents are against seeking help. In these cases, the parents have not yet accepted alcoholism as a disease. They may feel ashamed of the problem at home. They may think that by keeping the problem quiet and acting as if nothing is wrong, they will not lose face in the community. Moreover, your mother may feel the reason you want to seek help is because she has failed you as a mother—not because of alcoholism.

In these cases it is wise to send for brochures on alcoholism from the nearest Alcoholics Anonymous office, or from your nearest Council on Alcoholism, and show them to your parents. Perhaps you can convince your mother to go to the monthly open meetings of Alateen, where guests are welcomed. Very often a teenager will find that one or both parents are so bogged down by their problems that they do not have time, or a clear head, to think objectively about any organization.

If you do decide to go to counseling or to join Alateen

be careful that you do not let your parents feel you are seeking help for them. You are going for help because you know that alcoholism is a disease and because the pressures that come with the disease have hurt you, too.

13

Alateen

How did Alateen start?

Alateen is an outgrowth of Al-Anon. Al-Anon was organized by the wives and husbands of those alcoholics attending Alcoholics Anonymous. The purpose of both Al-Anon and Alateen is to help those living with an alcoholic regain their inner strength and stability.

Before Alateen existed, a parent was always encouraged to bring their teenager along to Al-Anon, but teenagers found it hard to discuss their problems at Al-Anon meetings when one of their own parents was listening. In 1957 a young California boy, who felt that the problem of the teenager with an alcoholic father or mother was different from the problem of the nonalcoholic wife or husband, founded a new group which came to be known as Alateen.

What actually happens when you join Alateen?

Alateen can change your whole life. In Alateen you can talk to other teenagers who also have an alcoholic parent. Alateens encourage one another and learn effective ways to cope with their problems.

Alateens air out their problems of living with an alcoholic. Each member realizes that other teenagers also have moments when it is difficult for them to act properly toward their ill parent. In talking to these teenagers, you will find that your personal experience can help them, too.

In all discussions, last names are never mentioned and specific personal acts are never described. The sponsor of each Alateen group who is an Alcoholics Anonymous member, Al-Anon member, or an understanding experienced Alateen member helps to lead the discussions. Alateens will sometimes have parents come from Alcoholics Anonymous to describe what they went through before they stopped drinking. This is always a marvelous opportunity to ask questions.

Teenagers who belong to Alateen never feel alone. They make new friends. When they visit each other, no one has to explain why a parent in the home is ill. In between group meetings, when things are rough at home, these teenagers can phone the group's sponsor or a fellow member to discuss the immediate problem without interfering in the parent's way of life. For example, if a member has a geometry exam to cram for, and a parent is drinking, an experienced Alateen member will not tell the parent to stop drinking, but will focus her concern on the fellow member. If he is upset, a fellow Alateen member might calm him by reminding him that the parent is ill and that the parent has to come to his *own* decision to do something about the drinking. If necessary she will get the teenager out of the house, and help to find a peaceful place to study, be it the library or another member's home. Should a teenager find the situation at home intolerable because a parent is abusive, a fellow Alateen member may offer her home until the parent sobers up.

Is that the whole Alateen program?
No. Aside from having a sponsor and meetings, they follow the same Twelve Steps as Alcoholics Anonymous and believe in living "one day at a time."

What is "one day at a time"?
"One day at a time" means that Alateens deal with each day as it comes. You can endure something for twenty-

four hours. There is always hope that the next day might be completely different. Alateens feel, why waste your precious energy worrying about the unknown when you can put that energy to use to make today better?

Do Alateens pray?

Like Alcoholics Anonymous, Alateens say they are a non-religious group. God is interpreted as each member sees Him.

I am exceptionally shy. I don't think that I could ever open my mouth at an Alateen meeting. When one goes to an Alateen meeting is one asked to say anything?

No one is asked to talk. But you cannot help but participate, because as others talk your reaction will be: "The very same thing happened to me," or, "Wait, let me tell you how I handled that same situation." You will develop an inner strength and confidence that you have never known before. Alateens plan fun, too. They have parties and barbecues which every member enjoys.

Where are Alateen and Al-Anon located?

They should be listed in your phone book under Al-Anon. Once you phone Al-Anon, they will tell you where the nearest Alateen is located. If you cannot find it in your phone book, write to Al-Anon, P.O. Box 182, Madison Square Station, New York, N.Y. 10159. If there is no Alateen group close to you, the main headquarters will tell you how you can start one. The main office in New York puts out a newsletter called *Loners' Letterbox* written for those teenagers who do not live within commuting distance of a community, or who are not well enough to go out. In this newsletter members share their experience, strength, and hope. Registered members will also correspond with such teenagers and share their meetings with them.

What do the mothers and fathers discuss in the closed meetings of Al-Anon?

These mothers and fathers discuss in part how to have better relationships with their children, how to have greater compassion for their sons' and daughters' experiences with alcoholism, and how to help the alcoholic realize that she is ill, or, if she has stopped drinking, how to give support.

Does the fact that the nondrinking parent goes to Al-Anon and the children to Alateen have any effect on the drinking parent?

Quite often it does. When the alcoholic sees the family pull themselves together and treat him with the knowledge that the compulsive drinking is a sickness, he may be motivated to seek help.

I get discouraged very easily. My father admits he is an alcoholic, but he has not stopped drinking. All these Alateen life styles sound great, but how can I believe them when I see what goes on at home?

Go to Alateen and you will find out it is possible to change your life. At each meeting you get new courage, more insight on how to handle your problems, how to cope with your sick parent, and, above all, how to manage your personal life.

At one Alateen meeting a girl pointed out, very sadly, that her father had gotten drunk again just when she thought he was going to make an effort to seek help. She also told the group that when he was recovering from the drinking bout, he talked to her as he had never talked to her before. He mentioned that he now considered his drinking an illness. Another girl at that Alateen meeting, whose father had not touched a drink in two years, explained to her that things were not as glum as she thought. The fact that her father admitted that he was ill was a real step forward on his part, and she assured her that her father would eventually seek help. She pointed out that she should give her father more courage and more hope.

To believe Alateen works, you have to go and experience it.

Suppose my father never stops drinking?

As you are growing up, you will make more and more friends outside of your family, you will date more, and, in all likelihood, you will form a family of your own. You will have your career, your place to live, and you will be able to separate yourself from the problems at home. When you think of it, most children only spend eighteen or twenty years at home. They are important years because they are your formative years. But now that you are aware of what makes you tick and of people who want to help you, you can take the fruit of your experiences, the tough things you saw, as well as the positive and constructive experiences, and build them into the kind of life you always wanted for yourself. To help you along in adult life, you may want to join Al-Anon, Adult Children of Alcoholics, or other support groups.